Everybody has a SUNFISH STORY

Stephan J. W. Platzer

ISBN: 978-1-959102-29-8

EVERYBODY HAS A SUNFISH STORY

Second Edition

Copyright © 2016, 2023 by Stephan J. W. Platzer

All rights reserved. Except for use in any review, the reproduction or utilization of this work in whole or in part in any form by any electronic, mechanical or other means, now known or hereafter invented, including xerography, photocopying and recording, or in any information storage or retrieval system, is forbidden without the written permission of the publisher, Bellastoria Press, P.O. Box 60341, Longmeadow, MA 01116.

Second Edition

Cover photos courtesy of Donna Burall, Linda Cardillo and Stephan Platzer.

BELLASTORIA PRESS
P.O. Box 60341
Longmeadow, Massachusetts 01116

DEDICATION

I would like to dedicate this book to my parents.

Where would I be without them?

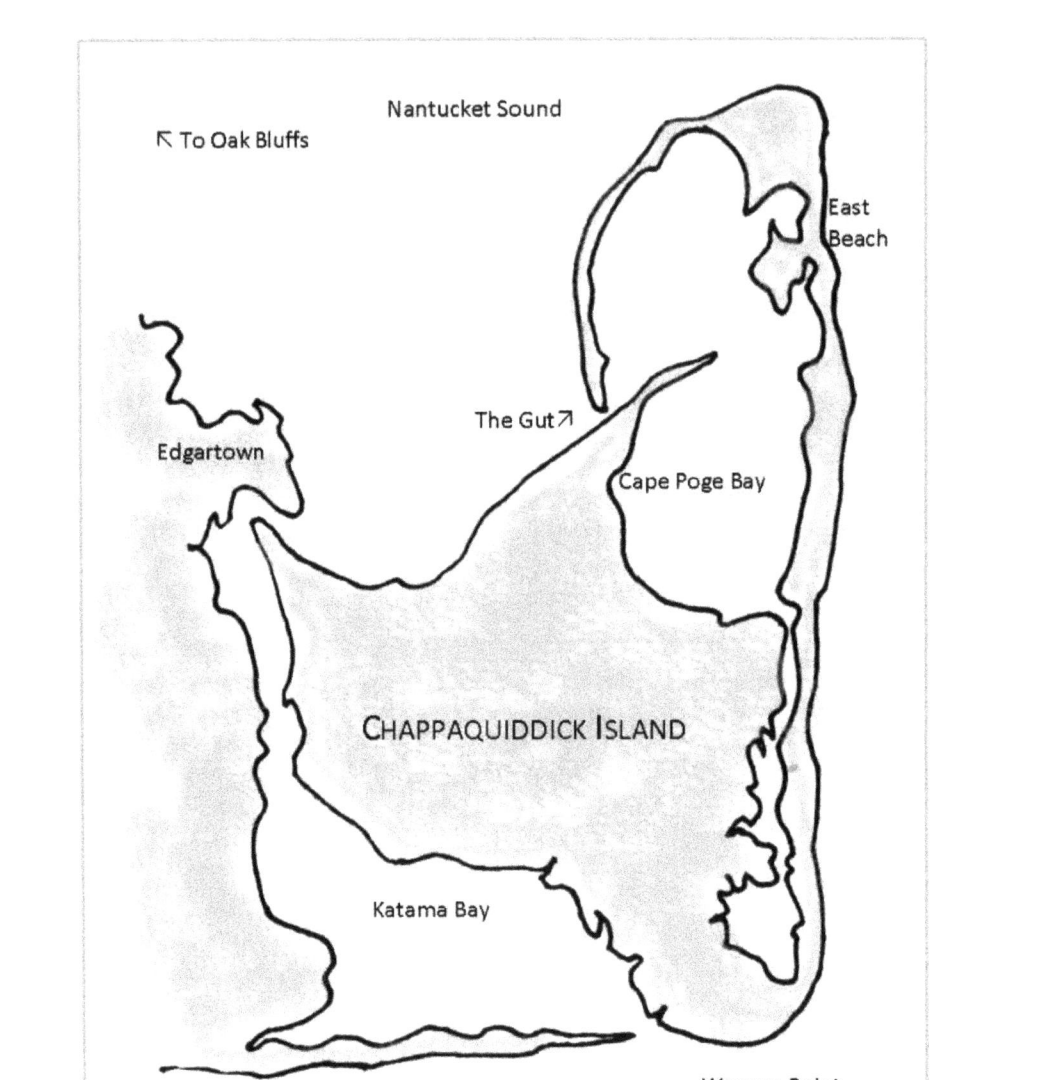

23 They that go down to the sea in ships, that do business in great waters. . .

27 They reel to and fro and stagger like a drunken man, and are at their wits' end.

From Psalm 107

And when the big wheel starts to spin,

You can never know the odds.

If you don't play, you'll never win.

From "Sun & Moon" by Above & Beyond

Table of Contents

		Page
Introduction		9
Acknowledgment		13

The Stories

1953	Sunfish Origin – *Steve Burrall*	25
1958	A Wooden Kit – *Chips Norcross*	29
1963-65	A Collegial Crew – *Steve Burrall*	33
1964	Sunfish Flirtation – *Michael Platzer*	39
1966	A Sunfish Romance – *Sandy B*	43
1973	Dead Reckoning – *Jim Sturges*	49
1982	Watch Out for Muskrats! – *Luke Platzer*	55
1983	Sunfish High on Lake Carnegie – *Stephan Platzer*	59
1986	Rocking the Boat – *Chris, the Mail Carrier*	63
1988-93	A Five-Year Gift – *David Schweidenback*	69

Table of Contents (continued)

1995-99	Big Fish on a Small Sunfish – *Chris Platzer*	77
2002	Aim for the Pine Tree Across the Pond – *Linda Cardillo*	87
2002	Sunfish Swimmer – *Eva Andrei*	91
2004	Lost in the Fog – *Mark Platzer*	93
2004	The Poetry of the Ocean – *Amelie Levine*	97
2005	Crowded Boat – *Mike Morehardt*	103
2007	A Grand Day Out – *Nicola Platzer*	109
2011	Circumnavigating Chappy – *Steve Brown*	113

INTRODUCTION

My father sailed on the Mattsee in Austria with his brother, Wilfried, who was older and the boss/captain of their boat, called Willy II. Wilfried later became the Austrian ambassador in Washington, D.C., during the Kennedy era, and in London thereafter; whereas my father received his Ph.D. in organic chemistry from the University of Vienna in 1936 and completed his chemical engineering studies at the Imperial College in London in 1937. My father's first job was in a chemical factory on the border between Austria and Germany, working on the latest polymers. One day he was on a train to Munich and spotted a beautiful young woman sitting with her mother. He did not say a word to the woman of interest, but did ask the mother if he might have a date with her daughter. She gave him the contact information. And so started their relationship.

My mother was born in the "miracle" town of Altötting, in Bavaria, where pilgrims still make the journey to pray for cures for the sick and injured. Her father, a physician from a family of accomplished medical doctors and the chief surgeon in the town, was often called upon to certify miracle cures. My mother's parents had a vacation house on the Chiemsee, one of the biggest lakes in Germany, with the snow-covered peaks of the spectacular Alps in the background. And they had a sailboat. Her brother and/or boyfriends did the sailing while she would be the person in the bow sunning herself. If no wind, she would sun herself on a boulder in the lake, pretending to be a mermaid. The lake has three islands: Herreninsel (gentlemen's island), Fraueninsel (ladies' island), and Krautinsel (cabbage island). (As children, we often told the joke about men and women getting together on Krautinsel to make "cabbage patch kids.") She was 22 years old and an art student at the University of Munich when she first met her future husband, who was 11 years older. The year was 1942, during World War II.

    My parents were married after a year of dating. My father sold Willy II to buy furniture for their new home, an apartment among many located within Burghausen Castle, which is the longest castle in the world. My mother had to promise her father that she would not have any babies during the war, due to the bombing and food rationing. Shortly after the war, in 1946, my older brother was born. My grandfather then requested that they refrain from having another child until Germany had recovered from the war. My parents had a nursemaid to take care of their newborn child while they got to enjoy life again, by going sailing on the weekends. One weekend they rented a boat and a hotel room on the Wolfgangsee, across the border in Austria. A beautiful day with a good breeze. However, a storm with pouring rain and strong gusts came quickly and nearly capsized their sailboat. They hurriedly sailed back to the home port, tied up the boat onto the slippery dock, and rushed back soaking wet to their warm hotel room. Well, nine months later I was born. This might explain my passion for sailing.

After World War II, my family moved from Germany to the United States and settled in Massachusetts. When I graduated from Cranwell Preparatory School in the Berkshires in 1966, my parents gave me a used green Sunfish as a present. $500 with trailer. Serial No. 16268, built in 1964. They knew that I was going off to Tufts University, so the boat was really more for them than for me. That was 50 years ago.

Stephan J. W. Platzer

ACKNOWLEDGMENT

The Sunfish is the most popular sailboat on the planet. Twice as many Sunfish sailboats have been sold as compared to the closest competition. Its popularity has sparked an abundance of words to honor it, including:

"Once launched, it brings its occupants closely and swiftly to the glories of wind and water." –*The New York Times*, 1974

"The appeal of the Sunfish…cuts through a lot of social, economic and ethnic strata." –*Sports Illustrated*, 1982

In 2001, with more than 300,000 boats worldwide, the Sunfish's 50th birthday was celebrated in Newport, Rhode Island. And now, in 2016, we are celebrating the 50th anniversary of *my* ownership of a Sunfish. Much has occurred since I received it, but that Sunfish has truly remained a strong, vivid part of my life.

My Sunfish has been shared with many friends and relatives who presently range in age from 25 to 75 years old and who have agreed to tell their stories of the Sunfish. In addition, others have related their experiences on other Sunfish sailboats. I wish to acknowledge all the authors who have generously contributed to this collection of romantic, funny, and heartfelt stories, from one-liners to multiple pages. I got the boat when I was 18 years old and have now gathered a total of 18 stories. As an avid listener to StoryCorps on National Public Radio, I often encourage people to write down their version of a particular adventure and to share it with others. Obviously, this Sunfish has played a very important role in my life…and also in their lives.

Steve Burrall. The nephew of an inventor of the Sunfish, Steve grew up spending his summers sailing on Noyes Pond in Western Massachusetts, where the Sunfish first took to the water. Steve also worked in the Alcort plant for three summers while attending college. Neighbors of the Burralls were the Wallaces, and Phebe Wallace was kind enough to invite Linda and me to sail my Sunfish on this historic lake. Phebe's son Jock, at 8 years old, was the original poster boy for the Sailfish (the original sailboat from Alcort).

Chips Norcross. A generous friend, Chips is a 34-year teaching, coaching, and dorm-parenting veteran from the Fay School in Southborough, Massachusetts. He inherited a passion for sailing from his mom who, during the 1930s, sailed on Nantucket Sound with the Wiano Senior fleet. When the family moved to the Berkshires, it downsized its horizons to a three-Sunfish flotilla birthed on Lake Woronoco (otherwise known as Hazard or Russell Pond) where the family enjoyed many summers of spirited competition.

Michael Platzer. My older brother, Michael, was involved with the Model United Nations since middle school. By the time of his university years, Michael was a confirmed "internationalist" and pacifist. Upon graduation from Cornell Law School, he took a position with the United Nations and spent 34 years working for human rights; defense of women; environmental causes, including climate change; youth projects; criminal justice and prison reform; and the inclusion of the poor and vulnerable on a national level.

Sandy B. The story from Sandy B is based upon letters she wrote to me in the 1960s. The summer evenings we spent drifting and sailing together are among my fondest memories of the early years with my Sunfish.

Jim Sturges. My college sophomore roommate at Tufts University, Jim, has ocean water in his blood. He grew up in Hyannis Port on Cape Cod, where his father was a commercial fisherman. Jim spent his summers learning to sail, racing several types of sailboats, and participating in periodic cruises on larger sloops and yawls over to the islands of Nantucket and Martha's Vineyard. When he wasn't sailing, he worked for his father. While on active duty in the Navy, Jim was part of a winning East Coast Navy Sailing Championship team in Annapolis, Maryland. Since those early years, he has lived most of his life in Rhode Island, and still takes part in the annual Fools' Rules Regatta in Jamestown. His career has largely been with Raytheon, developing underwater acoustic devices and their support systems for the Navy.

Luke Platzer. My older son, Luke, went on to Harvard, where he rowed for Winthrop House. He is now a successful attorney in Washington, D.C. Luke has expanded his sailing experiences to chartering yachts in the Caribbean and the Aegean Sea with his close circle of friends.

Stephan Platzer. Although I began my sailing adventures on a Sunfish, I have since journeyed on larger vessels, such as a Viking replica ship from Norway to England; a yacht surrounded by icebergs in the

Greenland Sea; an 1890s schooner from Africa to Newport, Rhode Island; and a steel-hulled sailing ship around Cape Horn in their winter, traveling from east to west, against the wind and currents.

Chris, the Mail Carrier. My local mail carrier, Chris, made the mistake of stopping by for a chat one Saturday morning and got persuaded to contribute a tale from his teenage years. Names in the story have been changed to protect the not-so-innocent.

David Schweidenback. A former Peace Corps volunteer, David recycles bicycles and sewing machines to provide economic opportunity for individuals worldwide. The Rolex Awards for Enterprise 2000 Laureate and president and founder of Pedals for Progress realized how the simple bicycle could transform people's lives by improving productivity. Since its inception in 1991, Pedals for Progress has donated more than 146,000 bicycles to 35 developing countries.

Chris Platzer. The oldest of my younger brother Gregory's five children, Chris was behind the tiller of a sailboat from the time he was a toddler. He teaches auto mechanics at a technical college and keeps the extended family well-supplied with venison during the hunting season. My brother loved sailing and designed ship propellers for the U.S. Navy and large yachts. Unfortunately, Greg passed away at a young age. In memory of Greg, a propeller blade that he designed rests in my garden.

Linda Cardillo. In the spring of 2002, at a fundraising auction, my talented wife, Linda, won a week at a cottage on the remote northern tip of Chappaquiddick Island. We brought my Sunfish along with our three children, who initially were not thrilled by the lack of electricity (and therefore, no TV and no video games). But the serenity and beauty won them over quickly, and for the next 10 years, that cottage became our very special vacation home. Linda spent most of her time on the island writing, and the last three of her novels are a trilogy inspired by the beauty and history of the land on which the cottage was built.

Eva Andrei. Following her undergraduate degree from Tel Aviv University, Eva received her Ph.D. in Physics from Rutgers University. Her daughter and my son Luke went to the Livingston Day Care Center at the same time.

Mark Platzer. My younger son, Mark, has become the unofficial captain of my Sunfish, teaching his friends how to sail (including my technique of tipping over the boat in the early stages of the lessons so that his pupils learn quickly how to right it). An Ultimate Frisbee player at St. Paul's School, the University of Southern California, and in South Korea, Mark now spends his time composing and working in Tokyo.

Amelie Levine. A fellow commuter on my bi-weekly flights to North Carolina, Amelie endured my monologue about creating a book of

Sunfish stories and agreed to contribute her own memory of a Sunfish excursion.

Mike Morehardt. A lifelong friend of Mark Platzer, Mike was born and raised in Longmeadow, Massachusetts, where he was lucky enough to spend summers in Martha's Vineyard with the Platzer family. He resides in Superior, Colorado, and remains a close family friend.

Nicola Platzer. My athletic, marathon-running daughter, Nicola, was recruited by the women's rowing team during her first week at the University of St. Andrews in Scotland. Previously, she had been the captain of the cross country team at Longmeadow High School. The St. Andrews crew wanted her as the coxswain due to her strong drive to win (and her petite size). Nicola spent many cold mornings, with a warm mug of hot cocoa, telling the rowers to pick up the tempo, pull deeper. The team went on to win the Scottish rowing championship, thanks to her. She is now a physical therapist.

Steve Brown. My best friend, Steve, and I met on our BMW motorcycles in the parking lot between our buildings when we were graduate students at Rutgers University. He was in the Alcohol Studies Program and I was in the Chemistry Department. We discovered we were both from the Pioneer Valley in Massachusetts and our mothers knew each other. When I got married, Steve supplied a strawberry punch made with 180-proof alcohol, which he recreated to great acclaim at my 25th wedding anniversary. In 1982, Steve and I sailed across the Atlantic from Africa on the Schooner *Ernestina* (originally named the *Effie M. Morrissey*), the second-oldest ship in the United States. He passed away in 2018.

David Leone. In addition, I would especially like to thank David, who, with his wife, Beth Landi, edited this book. David wrote an article about my presentation on my transatlantic journey on the *Ernestina*: "The lecture was a hit with the crowd. That's because Platzer's book [*Bringing E Home*]—though dryly written as a diary of the voyage to sail an historic vessel across the Atlantic—is full of interesting anecdotes and semi-perilous situations. And Platzer's wit comes through both in the material and his retelling. For instance, an audience member asked how they preserved freshly killed hog on a boat without refrigeration. 'We didn't preserve it, we just hung it up,' he said. 'We're still alive. Some of us.'" –*The Wake Forest Weekly*, 2013.

SUNFISH ORIGIN

Steve Burrall
1953

Everybody, it is said, has a Sunfish story, and mine begins even before the "birth" of this ubiquitous boat. I was fortunate (mostly through family) to be involved in many of the incidents which led us to where we are today. My uncle was Alexander (Red) Bryan and my godfather was Cortland (Bud) Heyniger, who were close friends from Waterbury, Connecticut. They both loved to tinker and build things and started to work together after they returned from World War II.

After a couple of attempts at building a product which might be successful, Bud remembered seeing people surfing in Hawaii. His original thought was to put a sail on a surfboard (yes, he really wanted to build a windsurfer) but as they tinkered, the idea morphed into the first Sailfish. The Sailfish was a flat-decked boat and eventually came in two sizes; 12 and 14 feet long, with the larger one being more stable. These boats brought sailing to many people, as they were easy to transport and could be launched on lakes, rivers, or even in the ocean.

The business started out in a garage and the little boats were sold to friends in and around Waterbury. There was no dealer network and only a small production shop. Even the first "sales brochures" were produced locally with friends serving as the "models" for pictures. One evening, the boys decided that their little venture needed a name so they took the first few letters from each of their first names (Alexander and Cortland) and Alcort was born. Red was always the businessman while Bud was the builder who even appears in the instruction sheet for Sailfish and Sunfish kits, always looking dapper in his white shirt and bow tie.

As the business was growing, Red, a confirmed bachelor, met and married Aileen Shields, who came from a notable sailing family and was a recognized sailor in her own right. When she became pregnant and couldn't comfortably sit on a Sailfish, the idea of widening the boat out a little and putting in a small well for her feet was conceived. This, of course, became the Sunfish that we all know and love. The development did take some time and a few false starts. One modification was the replacement of aluminum dagger boards and rudders with the wooden ones used in the Sailfish.

A quality product and pride of craftsmanship were always paramount in the minds of Red and Bud. They also only hired people with their same passions and then treated them well (their first foreman, Carl Minot, stayed with the company for years). One day each summer, the shop would close down and everyone went out to a local lake for an outing. During the day, everybody went out on a Sunfish. For many of the workers, it was the first time they had been on any kind of sailboat, but the experience let them see fully what they were producing and how the final product worked. This served to increase the pride each member took in the job he did.

Our first Sunfish arrived one evening in 1953 on the top of Red's car. It was a beautiful white boat with a red cotton sail and I believe had the number "25" hand-stamped into the hull, which was how they were serialized at the time. To protect the mahogany trim, my dad put the boat on a couple of airbags, but unfortunately, failed to tie it to the dock. A wind came up overnight that lifted the boat off its resting place and threw it on the rocks. A rather inglorious beginning. Fortunately there was no damage to the integrity of the boat, and with a little plastic wood and paint she sailed for many years.

This ubiquitous little boat, born out of a couple serendipitous events, has become the largest and most populous sailing class in the world. But more than that, it has touched the lives of hundreds of thousands of people. Yes, everybody has a Sunfish story.

A WOODEN KIT

Chips Norcross
1958

As a 12-year-old during the mid-1950s, a Sunfish provided me with one of the very few projects I ever helped my dad complete. He was a devoted physician with little time for family activities; however, a wooden Sunfish kit was too great a temptation for him to ignore. The kit combined his fascination with woodworking and an opportunity to provide my mother and the whole family with an easily transported craft for lake sailing (my mother grew up as an avid sailor).

Unpacked in the basement of our home, we spent several months assembling, gluing, screwing, sanding, and painting the Sunfish to make it ready for its maiden sail. When it was complete, we got ready to haul it out of the basement and up the steep staircase to the outside. There was just one problem: It wouldn't fit!

To gain maneuvering room to haul our new creation up a steep staircase, we had to remove several courses of brick from the basement bulkhead.

Our brand new Sunfish had its inaugural sail in Russell Pond, Massachusetts, otherwise known as Lake Woronoco. She was christened the *Ximena* in honor of the wife of El Cid of Spain (a legendary family ancestor). For at least a dozen summers, she was one of a fleet of three Sunfishes which competed in frequent formal and informal races, with cheap hand-painted ceramic mugs often presented to victorious skippers. Reading the fluky lake winds, sailors of all ages had a chance to demonstrate their strategic skills.

Sunfishes provide their crew with an incredibly close proximity to the water, giving an opportunity to intensely experience an essential element of our environment. Often this intimate interaction brings a lifelong respect and appreciation for the complex dynamics of rivers, lakes, and oceans. As variable winds interact with changeable currents and tides, one learns how to navigate a purposeful course. Many Sunfish sailors have a personal connection with this life-enriching process.

Over 60 years have passed since our Sunfish first set sail. Our family's life journeys have gone in numerous directions. For the past 40 years, the *Ximena* has quietly rested in a corner of our family farm's field. Dreams of trying to fiberglass her leaky hull have come to naught. Recently I became aware that a local family had a fiberglass Sunfish hanging in their garage, one which had not been in the water for at least several dozen years. After brief negotiations, I now own the *Ximena II*. As part of my retirement activities, I look forward to introducing local friends to the joys and challenges of Sunfish sailing.

A COLLEGIAL CREW

Steve Burrall
1963 – 1965

During the summers of 1963-1965, I had the opportunity to work on the factory floor of Alcort, Inc. While this was great summer employment, it convinced me that I wanted to finish my college education and move on.

During this period the atmosphere throughout the company was extremely collegial. The entire crew worked hard and always with the thought to put out a quality product in which everyone could take pride. The smallest blemish or a part not fitting quite right was cause for that boat to be deemed a "second." This atmosphere, fostered from the top echelon, permeated the entire shop and everyone bought in. The emphasis on quality was also reflected in all the materials used. There was no scrimping to save a few dollars. Only mahogany was used in all rudders and dagger boards as well as the trim on the Sailfish and the original Sunfish. Corks were imported from Portugal. Everything was first rate.

I made many friends and learned new skills, although being the boss's nephew gave me a few additional hurdles to overcome. Eventually I was accepted, however, and worked through several departments. I was actually there to learn the business from the bottom up with the thought that I might come join the company in the future. That never materialized, but I had a great education.

My first job was to work making masts and booms. These may seem like a small part of the boat, but the process to make them showed how seriously the company took all aspects of the product. Think for a moment what one of these spars really is. They start out simply as aluminum tubes. Since they will be subject to many stresses, the first process was to test them to make sure they met the appropriate specifications. Tubes that didn't measure up were immediately scrapped.

Next came the process of attaching hardware. We had a tube through which we had to drill holes (no pop rivets in those days) and which we wanted to remain watertight. The solution to this dilemma was to place a cork in each spot where a hole would be drilled to attach a block or other piece of hardware, plus one at each end. The method and tools for doing this were developed on the fly by the people involved.

First came the corks. These were all shipped in from Portugal in big bags. Larger corks for masts and smaller ones for the upper and lower booms. The corks had to be soaked in water for at least 24 hours in order for them to become soft enough to work with. The appropriate tubes would be laid out on a wooden bench of the proper length. An aluminum collar had been devised which would squeeze the wet cork from its current size to the size needed to go into the tube. The end of the tube was coated with wax and the cork was pounded through this collar with a mallet and pestle type of apparatus which got the cork into the tube (often resulting in a blood blister from hitting it wrong). Once the cork was in place, it was pushed into the tube by a rod into which one could put a bolt at various places to properly position the cork.

Once all the corks were in place for the particular job, we had to drill the holes in the proper place. These were properly marked, but drilling a tube is not easy and takes a lot of practice to keep the drill from running off from its intended spot. There were a lot of unfinished masts and booms that were scrapped as I learned this particular skill. Finally, caps were placed on each end to seal the booms or mast.

My second and third summers were easier, as I was a known quantity by my fellow workers. I moved around to other areas learning the anatomy of the boats and other skills. To this day I get a little nostalgic whenever I smell fiberglass resin or fiberglass dust.

After I left, a union was voted in by the workers and largely as a result of this, the business was sold to the industrial conglomerate AMF.

After my stint in the Air Force, I had an opportunity to return to AMF Alcort for a special project. I found the atmosphere and attitudes were entirely different from earlier days, but I did have a chance to catch up with some of my friends from my previous employment and relive the days of working for Alcort, Inc.

SUNFISH FLIRTATION

Michael Platzer
1964

As randy teenagers, my best friend Roger and I thought the best way to attract chicks was to offer them rides in our brand new twin Sunfishes.

We would load up our "fishes" atop our cars and head for Candlewood Lake in Connecticut. We had noticed beautiful blondes in bikinis in the cockpits of other Sunfishes on the lake and thought we could offer a similar experience to pubescent adolescents.

The offloading of Sunfishes was always an awkward thing for two scrawny teenagers, and we rarely paid attention to whoever was around during the unloading process. This was our big mistake. Because once we were flying across the lake, we rarely came ashore. We would race our boats across the lake, using all our sailing skills to best the other. Roger usually won because he had a newer boat. By this time, we were bored and scoured the beaches for sexy babes to join us on our "racing machines." We waved, yelling if anyone wanted a ride. Either we were not clear enough (or perhaps too obvious), too scrawny, or the girls simply preferred motorboat men. I must admit our adolescent flirting techniques even on shore lacked a certain *savoir faire*.

So in the end, we always struck out. We cursed the motorboats and praised the superiority of sailboats over stinkpots. What did girls know about the elegance of quietly sailing before the wind—especially in a Sunfish that was flush with the water.

My mother finally rescued me and organized a date with the daughter of a family friend. She was not blonde, but a brunette—but not without her charms. I was looking forward to this assignment and I gathered she was as well, as she had her hair done in a very expensive salon. However, when she saw that the Sunfish was not a big sailboat or a motorboat, she was disappointed. First, she was nervous, as Sunfishes are very tippy when you first get in. I helped her aboard. Then my memory goes blank. Either then, or shortly after we started sailing, the boom came flying over and knocked my prospective sweetheart into the water. She went under, her beautiful hairdo ruined, black hair running in streaks over her face. BB (she shall remain nameless) was furious. She sputtered out her anger about the cost of the hairdo. Despite reassurances on my part that tipping over and falling into the water was part of the fun and that she still looked great, BB never spoke to me again.

In the previous summer of 1963, Michael spent a month learning to sail at the Chiemsee Yachtschule in Germany, while I got to pick shade tobacco in the Pioneer Valley in Western Massachusetts. When he came back from Europe, we did a family road trip, mainly to look at possible colleges for him. We spent two days at the Lakeside Motor-Inn in Lake Placid, New York. While we were there, we sailed a rented green Sunfish, with Michael at the tiller and me holding the rope. Little wind. He then decided that he wanted to sail by himself and show everyone what he had learned at the Yachtschule. And I decided to borrow another Sunfish, for a little competitive sailing. We sailed back and forth, with me always winning. He then signaled that we should exchange boats, because mine was faster. Well, I continued to win. He announced that my advantage was my lighter body weight, not my natural nautical abilities. Well, he did eventually go to Cornell University in Ithaca, New York, living on Cayuga Lake (the longest Finger Lake). – Stephan

A SUNFISH ROMANCE

Sandy B
1966

"I do hope we can get to go sailing one last time—after all, where would we be if it hadn't been for your Sunfish."

The following is based upon the letters written by Sandy B to me. In those days, I was known as Steve. –Stephan

I wanted Steve when I first saw him. He was with Kathleen, my classmate from Ursuline Academy in Springfield, Massachusetts. And I was with his best friend, Rob. Steve and Rob were buddies from Williams Middle

School in Longmeadow, where Rob's mother taught English and loved to read Edgar Allan Poe poems. Steve went off to Cranwell Preparatory School, whereas Rob went to Monson Academy. The four of us were at the St. Nicholas winter dance, just before Christmas, in 1965. Steve and Rob were seniors, and Kathleen and I were sophomores in high school. Steve was a better dancer than Rob. He preferred slow dancing, namely, when he could hug his partner tightly. Rob told me that Steve was voted best-looking boy in the 8th grade, which made me want to be with him even more.

In June of 1966, when Steve graduated from Cranwell, he rode his bicycle from Lenox to West Springfield, about 50 miles, to impress Kathleen. However Kathleen was already in a serious relationship with someone else. She was not impressed. He was disappointed. As a graduation present, Steve's parents gave him a green Sunfish. This was my golden opportunity to capture him, because I lived near a lake in Ellington, Connecticut, only 10 miles away from Longmeadow.

Steve had a summer job cutting grass at his "beloved" Longmeadow Country Club. His favorite place to work was the putting green by the club's swimming pool. He was easily distracted. It took him at least twice as long as normal to do that job. I knew then that I had to seduce him away from the beautiful, rich, bikini-clad girls. However, I was built like Twiggy (an extremely thin model famous in the 1960s). I tried on many bikinis but none fit my slender body. I had to resort to a one-piece bathing suit. My mother told me that I had to stand up straight; otherwise one could see my breasts when I bent forward. She did not say anything about sitting up straight. (It is nearly impossible to sit up straight on a Sunfish.)

After work, Steve hitched up his Sunfish on a trailer to his mother's VW Beetle. He then picked me up at my house and drove to Crystal Lake, a gorgeous, small lake with a length of roughly a mile, with very few motorboats. We had the Sunfish in the water by 4 in the afternoon. The wind was usually strong then, requiring that we both sit on the upwind side of the boat. Our bodies, clothed in bathing suits, would occasionally touch in the summer heat.

Around 5 o'clock, the wind was not as strong. Steve asked me to sit on the downwind side of the boat while he was on the upwind side. Due to the tilt of the boat, I had to bend forward, towards him. I believe that he enjoyed the view down my top, because he said that it was his favorite time of the day. He often had a lovely smile on his face.

Around 6, the wind died down further. Steve called that time of day the "evening doldrums." It was the time when we could talk, as we sat up straight on opposite sides of the Sunfish. I quickly figured out why he loved to tack into the wind, with the metal pole swinging back and forth. I never said, "Where?" when he said, "Duck!" I just bent forward to avoid the metal pole hitting my head, so that he could have another glimpse.

Over the summer months, my teasing bathing suit led to making out in the back of the VW Beetle in secluded woods off the main road, and then back to my parents' house. Kissing, touching, undressing, and ultimately "going all the way." The first time for me and for him. All due to a Sunfish … and two teenagers who fell in love that summer.

We stayed together for four years, with many ups and a few downs. The love letters stopped in 1970. –Stephan

DEAD RECKONING

Jim Sturges
1973

In the mid-70s while attending graduate school for engineering at the University of Rhode Island (URI), I met and befriended a fellow engineering student named Hugo. He was arguably a bit eccentric, as he would do things on occasion just because someone told him it couldn't be done. An example would be when he hiked to the bottom of the Grand Canyon and back and then down again in the same day. Or when he pedaled a bicycle across California's Death Valley. Both of these treks occurred on typically hot summer days.

In the spring of my first year at URI, Hugo mentioned that he would be bringing his Sunfish sailboat from his parents' house on Long Island to URI to use for the summer while conducting his thesis research. His plan was to drive to New London, Connecticut, take the ferry across Long Island Sound to Orient Point, catch a ride to his parents' house where the boat was stored, sail it back up Long Island's inner bay to Orient Point where he would camp for the night, and the next morning he would sail it across to New London (a distance of 22 miles), where he could strap it to his car and drive back to URI.

I volunteered to accompany Hugo for two reasons—it sounded like fun, and, after getting to know Hugo's background, I sensed that his nautical perspective could, at times, benefit from a second opinion. In any case, two heads would be better than one.

On the chosen day, getting to Long Island per the plan presented no issues. However, arising from camp the next morning on the beach at Orient Point, we were presented with thick fog—not an uncommon occurrence for this area in late spring/early summer. Waiting another day was not an option, as we both had commitments the following morning. The good news was that the tidal flow in Long Island Sound would be consistent and running east until late morning, and the breeze was a steady 10 knots or so out of the northeast. Years of sailing and other maritime experiences told me that, on a close-hauled starboard tack, the combination of tidal flow and wind would result in a true course close to northeast toward New London, to which Hugo agreed. On the other hand, if the wind changed direction or dropped off sufficiently, there was a chance we could end up on Block Island, or if we made a mistake and headed out to the open sea, even Portugal, for that matter. Estimated sailing time for the wind conditions was 3-plus hours, so waiting for the fog to burn off beyond about 8 AM was not an option.

 Getting underway in the thick fog was uneventful but somewhat unsettling in that we were sailing without any distant reference points or anything else visible within about 30 or 40 feet of the boat. Of course, a compass would have been good to have, but somehow that never made it onto the list of supplies to bring on board. The breeze gave no indication of changing direction or velocity, so we remained confident of reaching the Connecticut shore, even if it wasn't New London. After perhaps an hour of sailing, we heard the voices and laughter of others on a passing sailboat, but could not see them. Further along, the sound of a bell buoy came and went, again without visual contact. The apparent close proximity to the bell buoy was encouraging, as there was one approximate to the intended course. Other than the sound of one more boat passing, the only noise for hours was the wave slap on the windward gunwale of the Sunfish.

We passed the time by talking about some shared engineering interests, discovering a mutual interest in backpacking, joking about not knowing a word of Portuguese, and making bets about how far from New London we would come ashore. As we started coming up on the estimated time of passage, we fell silent, each of us honing all available senses to detect some indication of landfall.

After what seemed like an eternity, a small boat came into view, tied up at a mooring with a family aboard engaged in bottom fishing. Their response to our where-are-we query was New London's inner harbor!!! Thoughts analogous to repayment for all our years of making positive contributions to society entered our minds—someone was looking out for us after all. After telling them where we started, we couldn't tell whether they thought we were nuts, or they just didn't believe us.

At any rate, feeling our way along the Connecticut coast to New London would not be required, and there was no need for a single word of Portuguese—actually a bit of a disappointment for the adventurous side of our nature. Our nautical reckoning had been on target, and the Sunfish made it easy to hold our course direction and maintain ample speed.

We loaded the Sunfish onto the car roof rack and arrived back at URI uneventfully. Perhaps as a result of this adventure and our discussions, Hugo and I have since shared in some long-distance backpacking treks, and have stayed in touch for over 40 years.

WATCH OUT FOR MUSKRATS!

Luke Platzer
1982

My earliest memory of the Sunfish is from when we lived in New Brunswick—when I was around four years old. I remember Dad taking me and Mom out on the Sunfish to a lake near Rutgers University campus. (Based on later internet research and looking at photos 32 years later, I think it might have been Farrington Lake in New Jersey.) I had a small orange life vest on and it was a clear sunny day.

Along the edge of the lake there were a lot of areas of mud, roots, and aquatic plants. As we sailed by, Dad pointed to areas of mud and sticks and told me that was where muskrats lived. As a four-year-old child, I didn't quite know what a muskrat was, but thought it was something scary—like a bigger, scarier version of the rats I had seen in cartoons, except that it could swim and would bite—so I was afraid of getting too close to the shore.

    Not long after, Dad took too sharp a turn with the boat, and we tipped over on our side. It was a calm and still lake (and Mom and I were both wearing life jackets), so we weren't in any danger, just wet and uncomfortable, holding on to the side of the boat after falling into the lake. I remember being very scared—both because I thought we were going to sink (I didn't understand how boats worked yet) and because we were starting to drift towards the shore, where I was certain we were going to be bitten by the muskrats whose nests Dad had pointed out earlier. No one else seemed worried though. I remember Mom looking bored and a little annoyed at our predicament while Dad mainly just looked embarrassed as he worked to try to set the boat upright again. Eventually he got the boat back upright before we drifted all the way to shore, and were able to get back on, wet but unharmed, and sail back to where we had put in.

I don't remember going back to that lake again after that.

SUNFISH HIGH ON LAKE CARNEGIE

Stephan Platzer
1983

I bought my first house when I was a graduate student at Rutgers University in New Brunswick, New Jersey, with a job on the horizon. I made sure that I had a garage to store my Sunfish. To keep the costs down, I had two Greek roommates, one of whom got his pilot's license to sail yachts in the Aegean Sea and now owns part of a small island there. A good friend whom I do not visit often enough.

Shortly after I graduated, I went to my 10th reunion at Tufts University, where I met a charming fellow classmate, who had dated my freshman roommate. With Italian roots, she was living in the North End of

Boston, running a successful catering business. Whenever I visited her I got to peel potatoes and clean up the mess. Not very romantic. (She has since become a writer, and her novels are a lot more romantic.)

Eventually, I convinced her to move down from Boston with her young son, Luke, to be with me. We got married and have been together for more than 40 glorious years.

My house was only 15 miles from the northern tip of Lake Carnegie, which is manmade and shallow; in other words, not dangerous. Luke and I visited the lake often, and sailed back and forth across the rowing lanes for the Princeton University crews. Many afternoons were without wind. We drifted around, trying to get out of the way of the rowers. One day we were yelled at by one of the coaches in his motorboat. I guess that sailboats don't always have right-of-way.

On a quiet day, we were the only boat on the lake. A hidden, small rowboat approached us. I steered the Sunfish away but the rowboat was faster. The man in the boat wanted to know if we wanted to buy some "grass." I pointed out to him that my son was only five years old. That did not stop him from lighting up and offering to share the smoke with me. I then said that I did not have any money on board, which was true (due to my fear of tipping over). He finally moved towards a racing scull at the end of the course, with an exhausted rower. Perhaps that rower needed a boast of "high" energy.

And that was our experience of drugs on the "high seas" of Lake Carnegie.

ROCKING THE BOAT

Chris, the Mail Carrier
1986

The New York Times published an article eight years ago, titled "In the Berkshires, Turning Back the Clock." It was all about living in the area of Otis, Massachusetts. Well, I wish that I could turn back the clock at least 30 years, to the one and only time that I was on a Sunfish.

In those days, Otis Reservoir was called Otis Lake by the locals. Back then, I was a junior in high school and a starring member of the hockey team. The head coach had a cabin on the lake, and one warm autumn afternoon he invited me for lunch on the deck. The coach's daughter was also there on that sunny day. She was a senior at the same high school.

After lunch, she asked me if I wanted to go sailing with her. I hesitated. Her father mentioned that there was not much wind, nothing to be afraid of. She persisted and I answered yes. So with her father's permission, we got the Sunfish off the lawn and into the water, and then rigged it. We changed into our bathing suits back in the cabin and then got into the boat, with her telling me where to sit and what to do, like "Pull the rope." She pushed us off.

We drifted around for about 30 minutes, away from the cabin. We chatted about fellow classmates while I got to admire the attractive person sitting opposite to me in her green one-piece bathing suit. But then suddenly, she stood up and started to rock the boat. Back and forth, harder and deeper. I was getting scared, panicky. I was not a good swimmer. And then the boat tipped over. Splash. She was holding onto one side of the upside down boat while I was on the other side. The water was freezing cold. Brrr. I asked her why she did that. She answered, "For the fun of it." She then told me to swim around to her side of the boat so that we could turn the boat right-side up. I did as I was told.

When I came around, I noticed that the top of her bathing suit was low, revealing her breasts under the water. I liked what I saw. Before I could say anything, she told me to grab a hold of the dagger board sticking out of the bottom of the hull, and to take my weight and swing the boat back over. To help, she raised her top half out of the water, revealing more. I found it difficult to concentrate. I was totally distracted. But we managed to tip the boat right-side up.

She complimented me on doing a great job. I thanked her. She noticed that I was staring at a particular part of her anatomy, and then she dared me to remove my swim trunks. I could not resist her seductive voice and again did as I was told. I swung my trunks into the cockpit. She then removed her bathing suit and likewise swung it into the cockpit. We were now totally naked in the water, as we hung onto the Sunfish.

She let go and swam away from the Sunfish. I could not resist and swam after her, watching her "tail." After a few strokes, she turned around and looked back at me. I saw panic in her eyes. I asked her what was wrong, what had I done that destroyed the mood. She screamed, "The boat is sailing away!!" I turned around and noticed that it was moving away from us. The wind had picked up. We both frantically swam after the boat and I finally caught the dragging rope. Whew. We were both exhausted as we hastily put back on our swimsuits and climbed on board. She looked at me, smiled, and thanked me for the adventure.

She again took command of the boat, telling novice me what to do. However, this time we sat on one side of the Sunfish due to the strong wind, and occasionally our bodies would touch. Hmm. We sailed only for another ten minutes, back to the cabin. As a reward for capturing the boat, I was hoping for a simple kiss when we safely landed. But her father was there waiting for us. He said that he saw the Sunfish tip over in the distance. He could not see much because we were so far away. My extremely lucky day. All thanks to a Sunfish.

This Sunfish story remained our secret during my high school days, because I did not wish to upset her older, much larger boyfriend.

A FIVE-YEAR GIFT

David Schweidenback
1988 – 1993

I always wanted a sailboat but I grew up on the poor side of town. We weren't on the other side of the tracks as we had no railroad, but we were on the other side of the Paskamanset River and the large swamp floodplain on either side. Before my father died we were at the beach every night fishing; after he died I rarely saw the ocean even though we were only five or six miles away from it. My town was totally split economically between the rich yacht club members and the rest of us in North Dartmouth, Massachusetts. Most beaches were private, so I swam in creeks and the Paskamanset. The thought of owning a sailboat was totally beyond any hope. I had one friend in high school, Scott Brooks, who occasionally took me out on his Sunfish in Apponagansett Bay. It was amazing.

My life moved on, I lived ever farther from the sea and the idea of owning a Sunfish had faded or even been forgotten. I was working as a carpenter in Western Jersey when Stephan offered me the use of his Sunfish while he was overseas. We transferred ownership and title because this is New Jersey—you can't do anything without paying a fee—and I promised to take good care of the boat until his return.

My wife and I were at a magical point in child-rearing; both kids were actually happy. My daughter, Rina, was around nine and my son, Lars, was about five years old. Both my kids liked being around the water and around boats but had never had one to use. I'm kind of large, around 200 pounds, but my wife is small, and my wife and two children together only weighed as much as me. The four of us were actually under the manufacturer's suggested weight limit. The next challenge was if we could all fit in the boat together and enjoy it.

We are very lucky in that we live only three miles from one of the most pristine freshwater lakes in New Jersey. Round Valley Recreation Area is a tremendous facility. They built the reservoir in an old quarry surrounded by steep granite hills. When the water laps up on the shore, it is hitting granite, not soil. The other reservoirs in the area were built over old clay cornfields and although the water is clean, it is a dark, murky brown. Round Valley, on the other hand, has crystal-clear water and you can often see more than 20 feet down. The reservoir is 220 feet at its deepest point and, as on the ocean, conditions can change very rapidly. Being built between high hills, the top of the reservoir water level is more than 100 feet above the surrounding land. Strong breezes, crystal-clear water, and close to home.

When we began taking the boat out, we seat-belted my wife and two children altogether in the front of our pickup truck (which pulled the Sunfish trailer) but as the kids grew, I wanted to just let them ride in the back of the truck much like I had done all of my youth. My wife refused to allow the kids in the back of the truck without seatbelts. When I get an idea, it doesn't take me too long to figure a good option and one afternoon as I was driving down the street, I saw a neighbor who was throwing away the removable seat from his van. It was worn but had working seatbelts. I mounted the seat to a piece of plywood which I screwed to the bed of the truck, and then I put chains through the armrests and through the top rail of the truck. I then had a removable seat with seatbelts that I could stick in the back of my carpentry truck when we wanted to go sailing. My kids were ecstatic, my wife less so.

 The first couple shakedown cruises were adventurous, both with my limited knowledge of sailing and the kids never being on a boat so small where our moving weight mattered. We worked our way through stops and starts, and I figured out how to get us out to beautiful spots only accessible by boat. We spent a couple summers sailing the green Sunfish around Round Valley and even vacationed at a campsite on the far side of the reservoir. It took two or three trips to ferry the family, then all of the necessities across the water. Being at the campsite was like stepping back in time 100 years; there was hardly any sound other than that of an occasional airplane or the intermittent sound of the commuter railroad blowing its horn as it arrived at the Lebanon station. Not surprisingly, the campsites are infrequently used due to the difficulty of getting to them.

As we got better at sailing as a family, my children started bringing friends along, so at times there would be six of us packed onto the small green Sunfish. We all enjoyed swimming on the far side of Round Valley, where we could have the pristine water almost all to ourselves.

With so many people on the Sunfish, it was sometimes hard with intermittent breezes to have any movement. My daughter developed a game to pass the time. There's a lot of freshwater seaweed growing along the shallow edges of the reservoir. Rina would drop a small piece of seaweed at the bow of the boat and then we would count off how many seconds it took for the boat to pass it. We knew when we were over 15 seconds it was going to be a long time getting back to the dock and the trailer. Other times, when the wind picked up, it was less than one second. We occasionally looked like an overladen refugee ship with the four kids and my wife hiked out on the high side and me, the heavy one, on the low side. I can remember fishermen shouting, "How many people do you have on that boat?" on a couple of occasions.

These were great days. We would fill my Playmate lunch cooler with a whole bunch of sandwiches and fruit, bring a big jug of iced lemonade and the whole family would go and play in the crystal-clear water on hot summer days.

Stephan returned to the United States at what was becoming a critical point in family sailing. My children were just getting too big for all of us to fit on the Sunfish. So we bid a sad goodbye to the little boat which gave us so many great family memories. We made more memories on our own boat, a 16-foot Precision which we all sailed until the kids went off to college. I am presently boatless but that has not stopped the family from continuing to spend quality time together on the water. In 2010 we all went to Turkey and sailed around the Turquoise Coast on a gulet that we rented with family and friends. More recently, my wife, son, daughter-in-law, and I rented a beautiful sailboat to spend 11 days sailing around the Galapagos Islands.

I do miss the Sunfish and I have thought about buying one as it is now just my wife and me. The boat is the perfect size for the two of us to just go out for a sail and a swim.

The Sunfish was a tremendous positive for my family and I will always be grateful for having been given that opportunity.

BIG FISH ON A SMALL SUNFISH

Chris Platzer
1995 – 1999

Growing up, boats were always part of my life. There are pictures of my brother (Karl) and me on Dad's Catalina as small children. Karl and I were obsessed with fishing and there are pictures of us with our red plastic fishing rods with yellow plastic hooks and yellow string trying to fish off the sailboat. I say "trying" because the hook and line were not even long enough to hit the water. We were three and four years old at the time.

    I remember Dad teaching Karl and me to sail. We were about seven and eight, and we had great imaginations. Dad borrowed Uncle Stephan's Sunfish, and on windy Saturdays and Sundays he would trailer it to Lake

Pearl in Wrentham, Massachusetts. Dad would take Karl and me out sailing together. Usually one of us would be in charge of putting the dagger board up or down, and the other would be in charge of the mainsheet. Once we were in deep enough water, he would let one of us control the rudder. Dad usually had his hands full telling me to steer the boat a certain way and Karl to pull on the mainsheet or release it. Interestingly enough, we never capsized. We were always scared to flip the boat. Dad had let us watch *Jaws* at the beginning of the summer and Karl wouldn't go in the pool as a result of it. The idea of a man-eating shark beneath the murky water was in the back of our minds and it added excitement to sailing.

 Dad got us to the point where he could tell me to pick a point on land (usually a house or something similar) and Karl would get the mainsheet adjusted properly and we would sail to that point. Once we got there, it was time to tack. The trickiest part of that is getting three people to duck under the boom at just the right time in a cramped Sunfish! Eventually we had a pretty good system and we got it down to the point of it being pretty smooth (smooth as in, no one catching the boom on the top of their head, or anyone getting kicked, elbowed, or head butted in the maneuver).

Karl and I were always intrigued by Dad's sailing stories. I asked Dad, "Have you ever flipped over in the Sunfish?" He said, "Only once. I brought a lunch with me and I started eating my lunch when the wind had died down some. As I was enjoying my lunch, a gust of wind came out of nowhere and flipped the boat over."

Eventually Karl and I got over our fear of great whites in Lake Pearl. Dad would take turns pulling us behind the Sunfish across the lake. When you're seven and eight, this is probably the most fun you can imagine. Dad would let one of us get in the water and tell us to hold onto the rudder. As the boat picked up speed, we would get pulled behind the boat hanging onto the rudder. Back then it seemed like we were going millions of miles per hour behind that Sunfish!

Most summers for vacation Mom and Dad would rent a house on Lake Sunapee or Lake Winnipesaukee in New Hampshire for a week. For Karl and me, this meant one week of fishing. For Dad, this was his time to unwind and relax, and a big part of this was the water and sailing. Up to this point the only sailing Karl and I had done was Lake Pearl in Wrentham, which is relatively small at 218 acres. Lake Pearl is also surrounded by hills which tend to block the wind and make it swirl. Mom and Dad would load up the van and trailer the Sunfish to our rental cabin in New Hampshire. After everything was unloaded, it was time to put the Sunfish in the water.

The trip that stands out most to me was during the first week of August 1995 to Lake Sunapee. Most of Lake Sunapee has steep sides and there are only about three public boat launches, all of which are on the west side of the lake. Dad decided to use the Sunapee State Park boat launch, which is towards the southern end of the lake. After Dad got the Sunfish off the trailer and rigged, he asked, "Do you want to go for a boat ride,

Chris?" I said, "Yes." Mom drove the trailer back to the house, and Dad and I set off in the Sunfish towards the rental house. Compared to Lake Pearl, Sunapee is huge. I had never seen anything like it and being in such a small sailboat seemed daunting to me at the time. I remember there was lots of wind and waves that kept breaking over the bow of the Sunfish. It was overcast and the wind was blowing hard. For a nine-year-old, imagine a scene out of *The Perfect Storm*. I knew I was in good hands with my dad and after about an hour and a half we made it to the rental house safe and sound. I remember feeling so out of place in the Sunfish on the big lake, with heavy winds and the ominous sky.

As the week progressed, the wind settled down and Karl and I began using the Sunfish as our fishing transportation. We would paddle the Sunfish around without the mast and sail. Lake Sunapee was much different from anything we were used to fishing. The water was clearer and the bottom of the lake consisted mostly of large boulders. This makes the perfect environment for smallmouth bass, and Karl and I were determined to figure out how to catch them. After a few trips to the tackle store we had everything we needed to go fishing. Karl and I would paddle the Sunfish around while trolling deep-diving Rapala lures. We caught some big fish; then again, when you're kids it doesn't take much to qualify as a BIG fish.

When we got home and told Mom and Dad about our fish, they didn't believe us—the typical fishing stories, every time you tell the story the fish gets bigger! Karl and I decided we needed to bring the next BIG fish home so they would have to believe us. The next morning we went fishing and within an hour Karl hooked a BIG bass. We plugged the drain hole in the Sunfish's foot well and used a bucket to fill the foot well with water. Once we had enough water in the foot well we unhooked Karl's bass and threw him in our new live well! As luck would have it on our paddle home, we caught another BIG bass and we put him in our live well, too. When we got back to the rental house, we had Mom and Dad come out to look at our catch. I think they were more surprised by how we turned the foot well of the Sunfish into a live well for our fish than the actual fish.

Mom took pictures of us with our fish before we released them. The Sunfish provided us with a great alternative to fishing off the shore. Karl and I fished out of that boat every day we were at Lake Sunapee.

The summer of 1999 Mom and Dad decided to go to Michigan for a family reunion on Mom's side of the family. They planned to rent a house on Lake Michigan for a week instead of going to New Hampshire. I was 13 at the time. Because the ride was so long and the trailer for the Sunfish was so old, Dad made a set of roof rails for our Ford Club wagon 15-passenger van. I was going to help him put Stephan's Sunfish on top of the van. Dad and I picked up the Sunfish, rolled it upside down and stood on our tippy toes with the 100-pound Sunfish above our heads and slid it onto the roof of the van. This is an important piece of Sunfish history because in the process, I hurt my lower back and it took years of strength training to stabilize whatever I hurt lifting the Sunfish above my head. Fond memories of Stephan's Sunfish!

Once we got to Michigan and the reunion was over, we went to the rental house on Lake Michigan. When I saw the lake for the first time, I thought it looked like the ocean. It was fresh water but you couldn't see across it! This made Lake Sunapee look like a puddle and Lake Pearl look like a drop of water. In front of the rental home there was a nice beach, which was very convenient for storing the Sunfish when we were not using it. Naturally, Karl and I were eager to do some fishing. The chance of catching a BIG fish in the BIG lake really got us excited. There was the possibility of catching a lake trout, salmon, or northern pike. None of these fish were easy to find back home. As we usually did when we took the Sunfish out fishing, we left the mast and sail, grabbed our rods and paddles, and headed out. The water was very clear and suddenly got deeper the farther from shore we went. Karl and I could see fish on the bottom, but we were not getting any bites. After fishing for about an hour, we decided we needed to go back and change our tackle and technique. It was about this time that we both looked back at the shore and realized how far out we had gone. The house looked like a small dot on the horizon. Karl and I had been so engaged in what we were doing that we hadn't paid attention to how fast the offshore wind was pushing us. We were glad that we looked up when we did.

Karl was sitting on the front of the Sunfish and I was sitting in the back. We both started paddling as hard as we could against the wind. I would guess that we probably paddled for 15 minutes without making much, if any, progress. Karl and I were now getting worried; it was getting late, we were far from shore, and we were fighting the wind. We decided our only chance was to get in the water and swim the boat back in. We both hopped in with our life vests on and began swimming and pulling the Sunfish behind us.

Fortunately, after about 45 minutes, we made it back to water we could stand in and dragged the boat back up the beach. We were exhausted but safe. Looking back on the situation, if we had had the sails, it would have been no problem to tack back and forth to get home. Unfortunately for us though, our bodies were acting like sails catching the wind and pushing us straight out with the wind. That was the most scared I can remember being on the water in my entire life. Karl and I still joke about it to this day.

Chris's father (my younger brother) borrowed my Sunfish for a few years. He updated the rudder mountings and advised me to replace the torn sail. Eventually, the bottom and cockpit also needed to be fixed. In 2011, I asked Boat Works in South Windsor, Connecticut, if I should repair the boat or get a new one. They responded by asking me what it was worth to me. I replied, "Priceless." The repair bill was $300. They were greatly impressed that such an old Sunfish still floated. –Stephan

AIM FOR THE PINE TREE ACROSS THE POND

Linda Cardillo
2002

I had never been on a sailboat until I met Stephan. Italian girls growing up in New York near Long Island Sound had relatives with cabin cruisers, not yachts. Even in high school, when I was invited to spend a weekend at the Marblehead summer home of my friend Carol, her brother took us for a ride in his Boston Whaler, not his sailboat.

So when we trailered the Sunfish to Carnegie Lake in Princeton in the summer of 1980, I was totally clueless.

Luke was bundled into a neon orange life jacket, and the green cushions that serve as "flotation devices" were still intact—not the frayed and patched-with-duct-tape lumps that still get taken along when we launch the boat.

I was not a particularly apt pupil on that first voyage, and, to my disappointment, I have not yet learned how to read the wind. Stephan has been a patient teacher, repeating lessons from year to year, even tolerating with admirable restraint my crashing the boat into a rotting pier on Cape Poge Bay.

In reflecting on my misadventures with the Sunfish over the last 36 years, I realized that I had actually learned one simple but important lesson in sailing. I remember vividly both Stephan's suggestion and the location of the lesson. We were in Shear Pen Pond on Chappy in the late afternoon.

"Find something on the opposite shore," he said, "and steer for it."

Across the water I saw a lone pine tree, a solitary, dark green sentinel shaped like an open umbrella. It stood in stark relief against the pale green, undulating sheaves of marsh grass.

I moved the tiller and the nose of the boat lined up with the tree. I realized pretty quickly that, unless I kept focused on that tree, the boat was going to drift away from my goal. The trip across the pond required a series of subtle corrections, always guided by that dark silhouette on the opposite shore. Stephan's instruction had been simple, but it was also incredibly powerful. It gave me a sense of control and accomplishment at a moment when I had been feeling neither when it came to sailing.

I'm still a terrible sailor. But if you put me on the tiller, I know what to do, thanks to Stephan. And when, in life beyond the water, I need to get to the other side of something, I just think about that tree waiting for me and guiding me from the far shore of Shear Pen Pond.

SUNFISH SWIMMER

Eva Andrei
2002

"I was toying with the idea of helping you sail the old green Sunfish in Spruce Run, for old times' sake."

I still remember vividly the first time sailing with Eva back in the 1980s. She was an avid, accomplished swimmer who swung her feet over the side of the Sunfish, plunged into the water, and swam around the drifting boat, exploring what was beneath the water's surface. Perhaps swinging off the Sunfish into the cool, calm lake water then motivated her to study flat surfaces, for she is now a physicist, investigating two-dimensional electronic materials. — Stephan

LOST IN THE FOG

Mark Platzer
2004

For ten years of my adolescent life, my family rented a house every summer on the island of Chappaquiddick, the eastern section of Martha's Vineyard. Each year we would spend a week in almost complete isolation from the modern world and amenities in a small compound of single-room houses, getting a taste of the simple life. One of the main staples of both entertainment and relaxation during these vacations was sailing my father's Sunfish in the waters around the house. The first few years my dad would take friends and family out, and whenever I was with him, he would let me steer. A simple task but engaging enough to make a young boy feel like he was contributing and having an impact on those in the boat.

One of the most profound moments in my nautical career was during our third year on the island on a gray and gloomy day. It was just my dad and I spending the afternoon on the Sunfish, and the trip was pretty indistinguishable from any other. We struggled to make it past the choke point of Shear Pen Pond, there were threats by Dad of flipping us over, and we passed the time with small talk about life and where to steer. Dad decided to take me out into the slightly larger body of water by our house and just as we started making headway away from the house, an ominous fog began to roll in. What started out as a mist that would shroud the far-off landmarks of beachside properties and lighthouses became an immense curtain covering everything beyond ten feet of the boat. My dad took this only as a challenge and laughed as my heart began to sink as I lost track of my surroundings. My only compass in the abyss was the direction of the wind, and the fact that it would be nigh impossible to head out into open water from the sheltered bay we were in. It was an incredible feeling to be completely isolated from the world like that. My universe became everything within ten feet; my dad, the boat, and myself were all I could be sure of in the world. We spent a few hours navigating around, occasionally coming within sight range of land and realizing we were hundreds of yards from where we thought we were. The air was cold and wet, and I soon could only focus on the threat of my dad at any point deciding it was time to throw the boat upside down and send me careening into the water. Luckily for me, he was more sensible than I expected. After being uncontrollably lost for the day, we managed to find the general direction of home and only missed by about 100 yards.

I'll never forget stepping out into the cold, damp void on that Sunfish, but in stark contrast to that, I'll also never forget how good it felt to have four walls around me, a warm blanket, and my mother's cooking in my stomach.

THE POETRY OF THE OCEAN

Amelie Levine
2004

It was a sunny, pleasant day in July. Accepting my friends' invitation to come for a weekend to Nantucket Island off the coast of Massachusetts was very tempting, almost irresistible. I had never been to this island before. It was a longtime dream of mine, and visiting cherished friends on a small, uncrowded island was simply impossible to pass up.

When I arrived, my friends greeted me on the ferry pier with open arms that warmed my heart. And then the weekend adventures followed.

The unspoiled, unhurried beauty of Nantucket was preserved by its remote location, accessible only by a ferry. My friends' home in Wauwinet was even more remote, reached by a dirt road. These hurdles, though, were nothing to those seeking inspiration in the island's taming, subtle, soul-comforting beauty. Its wooded forests, with crooked, short pine trees one can find only on Cape Cod; and its ocean beaches that poets, artists, and writers get drawn to, evoke that lurking, tantalizing spirit that, once experienced, is impossible to forget. The only cure is to experience more of its beauty and inspiration.

The waters around the island are a paradise for those who are avid sailors, those who are addicted to the mystery carried by the ocean shores, and those who are eager to leave the comfortable, safe shores and wander deeper into the unpredictable surroundings of the water.

Never before had I tried sailing. The invitation of my friends to sail on a small Sunfish and teach me how to sail was so exciting that it seemed almost surreal. I couldn't wait until the sun rose the next morning and that dream of mine would become a reality.

And it did indeed. Shortly after a light breakfast, my host offered to take me sailing. We embarked on his Sunfish and left the shore of the Head of the Harbor, located right next to the house, and accessible through an alley of blooming beach roses.

And now I had my first sailing lesson from a passionate, experienced, longtime sailor. I wanted to do well, to follow instructions of maneuvering the tiller precisely. I was afraid my friend would be mad at me for turning the Sunfish in a wrong direction. But he was friendly, patient, forgiving, and very encouraging. The waves were splashing over my bare legs and arms.

The sight of the land became more and more distant as we left the harbor and sailed out the inlet into Nantucket Sound. The serenity of the surrounding waters, the view of the horizon, the sensation of complete isolation from the land, the thrill of the unknown, the risk of the adventure and its unpredictability were consuming all my senses. I was transported to the mysterious, breathtaking world that only nature can provide—far from the mundane, materialistic, hurried pace of everyday life.

The ocean is an ultimate experience of that serene paradise, but one that is full of the excitement of the unknown. It is dangerous, unpredictable, wild, and only more and more tempting because it is ever changing. It is most dynamic, keeping anyone who dares to connect with it on the edge. Only mountains and their high peaks come close to matching the ocean in its beauty and exhilarating appeal.

As the sun began to disappear among the clouds, the splashing waves brought chilly sensations to my skin. After a while, the cold reached my bones and I began shivering. My friend immediately took off his jacket and tossed it to me. I will remember that kind gesture for the rest of my life. It got imprinted in my brain, as did the first sailing lesson on a small Sunfish.

An outdoor shower under the pine trees and the stars, and a hot dinner awaited us when we returned from this unforgettable sailing adventure.

The beach, the waters, the Sunfish, and the inviting hospitality of my friends will stay with me forever. Since that first sailing adventure, each visit to the ocean and the sight of a sailboat on a horizon reminds me of that unforgettable experience, putting me into a dreamy mood, with wandering thoughts and desires to connect to the unpredictable, so ever passionate, wild nature of the ocean.

CROWDED BOAT

Mike Morehardt
2005

It was our first visit to Martha's Vineyard and learning to sail the Sunfish was high up on our list of things to do, along with going to all the different towns, hanging out at the beaches, swimming, and taking night walks on the phosphorescent beach. We had heard from Mark how much fun sailing was and of the adventures he and Dr. Platzy had been on.

"You guys know that my dad is gonna have to put you guys through a test to see if you'll be good for sailing around the little bay in front of the house and out into the main bay," Mark had told us early on. We were intrigued and asked what this test was, but Mark wouldn't elaborate.

When it came time for Greeny (Mike Greenberg), AK (Akshay Kashikar), and me to learn how to sail the little Sunfish, I wondered why Mark opted out from going with us. Then I figured it had to have been because of this "test." I was a bit nervous and started nagging Mark about it. He finally caved right before we all got on the boat. "He's gonna flip you guys." I'm not sure if it was just me or all of us he told, but I was glad to know what was going to happen.

One thing I am sure of is the type of day that we chose to go learn about sailing. It was cloudy with a cool breeze and all I could think about was how cold it was going to be if Dr. Platzy decided to do his devious deed. We got in the Sunfish, which soon looked like it was going to capsize in only three feet of water with all four of us guys in it. We pushed off and Dr. Platzy proceeded to go through various turns and detailed instructions on how to make the Sunfish "work."

I think I barely paid attention. I was too busy thinking: "Maybe he'll do it now? . . . Maybe now? . . . Oh! there's a big wave, maybe now! . . .

Now?" I wanted to try to be on my toes and foil Dr. Platzy's plans by somehow jumping onto the side of the boat that was going to go in the air when it capsized. Then it happened! I failed and I got wet and Dr. Platzy, that bastard genius, won. But I understood why he had to do it and it was so much fun . . . after the shock of the cold water passed.

The second sailing incident I remember is when we decided that staying in our little protected bay was getting old and planned on going out across the open water to Oak Bluffs. By this time we all had some good practice on the Sunfish and were ready to take on a challenge. And a challenge is exactly what we got. All five of us—Mark, AK, Greeny, Dr. Platzy, and I—piled into the tiny little Sunfish and headed out toward the main bay. I noticed that the extra weight of Dr. Platzy (no offense intended) brought the entire Sunfish down closer to the water, but it wasn't a problem since the water in the protected bay was pretty calm. I didn't realize that it was going to be much different across the open water. We entered the sound, which was actually just a larger bay, and the waves were maybe two to four feet high, or at least felt like that. It was a little intimidating in a tiny Sunfish with what seemed like too many people, but with a strong wind from behind and Dr. Platzy's expertise, we made it to Oak Bluffs in one piece.

I got out of the boat and almost kissed the ground for making it, but really, even if we did capsize we would have been fine. We got some ice cream and headed back to the boat quickly because it was getting late in the afternoon and Dr. Platzy was sitting with the boat on the beach. We finished our ice cream and reluctantly piled back into the boat. We pushed off . . . and went nowhere. Tacking back and forth against a persistent headwind, we were too . . . fat. So we decided that it would be best if we unloaded some weight. AK and I got out on the beach and we all planned to meet up again in Edgartown; AK and I would get there by foot and Mark, Greeny, and Dr. Platzy by sea. I remember AK and I walked along the coast most of the way, where we saw kids and families having so much fun in the water and on the beach while we walked by on the asphalt, roasting our butts off in the middle of a bright and sunny summer day. AK and I finally reached Edgartown before Mark, Greeny, and Dr. Platzy. We were relieved because we could finally sit down, relax, and enjoy some shade. When the others finally arrived, I think both groups realized how exhausted we all actually were, but that didn't prevent us from talking about each of our experiences and laughing about the day.

Thanks for the great times Dr. P!

A GRAND DAY OUT

Nicola Platzer
2007

One of my most memorable times on the Sunfish was on Martha's Vineyard. I was training for the Maine Marathon and needed to run while we were on Chappy. There was no place to run out by Cape Poge, so Dad decided that instead we would sail to Edgartown and I would run back to the Cape Poge Wildlife Refuge.

We stored my sneakers and socks in a Ziploc bag and hid them to keep them dry during the sail from Shear Pen Pond to Edgartown. Having my sneakers on board meant Dad wouldn't intentionally tip the boat. We zigged along the Chappy coast, avoiding sailboats and motorboats much larger than ours. Occasionally, we had to get unstuck on sandbars. After what seemed like hours, we arrived on the private beach next to the Chappy Ferry. Dad didn't care a bit and pulled up on shore. It was midafternoon by this point and I can remember feeling my skin frying as we pulled onto the sand. I don't think I brought a water bottle. We dug out my sneakers and socks—they were dry! I quickly stored them away from the shore and helped push the Sunfish (with Dad on board) out into the harbor channel, where several ships were passing. We agreed to meet along the coast in the refuge. He would try to get to the entrance.

    Thus began my three-mile journey back to Cape Poge, running along the side of the Chappaquiddick and Dike Road, trying to avoid the SUVs and finding any shade I could. I recall the relief of shade running toward the Trustees hut. I walked across the bridge to the sand dunes and couldn't see Dad. The sun was blazing down and there was no water in sight. I decided I would walk along the beach on the bay side to see if I could catch Dad. Sneakers in hand, I began the slow walk along the beach, my muscles aching from the run and salt sticking to my skin from evaporated sweat. After about 20 minutes of walking, I saw a little green sail off in the distance. Was that a little fish I saw? I could see it coming closer to shore. Then I spotted Dad, in his bucket hat, coming for me. What a relief. He pulled up on shore and handed me a bottle!!! Water never tasted so good. Sneakers and socks back in the Ziploc bag, time to make it back to Shear Pen for dinner. We were greeted by delicious food after a grand day out.

CIRCUMNAVIGATING CHAPPY

Steve Brown
2011

Chappaquiddick Island, colloquially known as "Chappy," is a small peninsula and occasional island on the eastern end of Martha's Vineyard. Norton Point, a narrow barrier beach, connects Martha's Vineyard and Chappaquiddick between Katama and Wasque. Occasional breaches occur due to hurricanes and strong storms, separating the islands for periods of time. Most recently, the two were separated for eight years, from 2007 to 2015. —Stephan

The highlight of one of my visits to Stephan on Chappaquiddick was sailing entirely around the island. We originally planned to sail just to Edgartown. The wind was from the south, directly against us. We left after breakfast at 1:30 PM. I first had to make numerous phone calls to cancel my afternoon meeting, letting colleagues know I wouldn't be returning to Maine that day. The tide change was about noon, which meant that we would be fighting the current. We tipped over at the Gut with people watching (embarrassing) near where Lady Gaga was rumored to be building a home. I remember wishfully talking about being invited by her to see the new place.

Once we got to Edgartown, we sailed past the ferry into the harbor, where numerous sailboats were anchored. Then we decided to sail past the Edgartown town line into Katama Bay and through lots of motorboat traffic. The bay is nice, with many expensive houses. We then proceeded cautiously across the Katama breakers, where many people have drowned because of the unpredictable strong currents. Lifeguards on both sides.

The land was connected up until a few years before, but in 2011 Chappy was truly an island. The depth of the water at the Katama breach was very shallow, just enough depth for the Sunfish. I teased Stephan that the breakers were six feet high. Nope, only about one foot.

Once we got through there, we had the wind at our backs. Beautiful sailing in the Atlantic Ocean. Our only fear at that point was that the wind would die. Off in the distance we could see the green areas of the Cape Poge Wildlife Refuge. We swiftly sailed along East Beach up to the lighthouse. I kept kidding about stopping for a beer, as I waved to passing motorboats. "Sailors don't wave to motorboaters," Stephan told me. I had drunk some water before we left but I was getting thirsty. We'd already been on the water for over four hours and we'd brought nothing with us to eat or drink.

Once we reached the Elbow by the lighthouse, we had to tack into the wind directly into the big waves. We hugged the Elbow to minimize the beating of the old fragile hull into the waves. We tacked back and forth, nearly tipping over many times. Stephan had to teach me to let go of the sheet if we tilted too far when the bursts of wind hit us. Waves about three feet tall. Past the windmill house, aiming for the Lady Gaga site. Back and forth, tacking into the wind with Stephan on the tiller aiming for Edgartown, hugging the shore where the waves were less high. The cliffs by the Gut protected us from the strong wind and lessened the height of the waves. It took us almost two hours for this stretch. Sunfishes do not sail well into the wind, nor into high waves.

Finally at the Gut, we turned into Cape Poge Bay towards Little Beacon in the distance. With the wind behind us, we were on a New England sleigh ride, with the dagger board up, zipping down to the house—which, like many island cottages, had a nickname, the Jib. It probably took us less than 20 minutes to cover the same distance that had taken two hours in the opposite direction. While we were tacking into the wind, we thought of dragging the boat across the dunes, to cheat. The sun was getting lower on the horizon. But we wanted to do it right.

We finally reached our destination. I let go of the sheet, slowing us down, and Stephan turned the tiller so that we gently touched the shore. We quickly pulled the Sunfish out of the bay to a point above the high water mark, dragging it across the seaweed on the beach, which prevented the hull from being scraped by the stones. It was close to high tide. We could barely stand after sitting so long. We then brought up the gear (sails, mast, tiller, dagger board, and mainsheet). It was 7:10 PM. Six hours of sailing nonstop with only one tipover. We arrived safely.

I had spent most of the trip telling Stephan about my life. But I think he would have been satisfied with less talk. He prefers to relax and listen to the wind and waves, at least some of the time. As he told me, "It is quiet without you." But now he knows more about my political and family life in Maine.

Linda and Mark could see us sailing in the Bay from the Gut with binoculars. She thought that we had sailed to Oak Bluffs. Both she and Mark had warned us to stay away from sailing around Chappy, echoing the advice of Judy (the owner of the cabins). Too dangerous. Actually sailing to Oak Bluffs would have been even more dangerous across the wide open bay. Perhaps Stephan and I should have brought along life vests. Next time.

Author's Note

If you enjoyed this collection of memories, I'd love to know if you have a favorite story. Please drop me a line at:

info@bellastoriapress.com

or

Stephan J. W. Platzer
c/o Bellastoria Press
P.O. Box 60341
Longmeadow, MA 06116

www.ingramcontent.com/pod-product-compliance
Lightning Source LLC
Chambersburg PA
CBHW062024050526
44107CB00105B/867